Walking on Darkness

Walking on Darkness

Peter Dale Scott

Designed and typeset by The Sheep Meadow Press
Distributed by The University Press of New England

Cover image: from Petrarch's *Libro de Sonetti et Cancione col comento di Francesco Philelfo,* 15th century, Folio 110r

Author Photograph: Carolyn Merchant

Library of Congress Cataloging-in-Publication Data

Names: Scott, Peter Dale, author.
Title: Walking on darkness / by Peter Dale Scott.
Description: Rhinebeck, NY : Sheep Meadow Press, [2016]
Identifiers: LCCN 2016003512 | ISBN 9781937679644
Classification: LCC PR9199.3.S364 A6 2016 | DDC 811/.54--dc23
LC record available at http://lccn.loc.gov/2016003512

All inquiries and permission requests should be addressed to the publisher:

The Sheep Meadow Press
PO Box 84
Rhinebeck, NY 12514

Books by Peter Dale Scott

The Politics of Escalation in Vietnam
    (1966, with Franz Schurmann and Reginald Zelnik)
The War Conspiracy (1972)
The Assassinations: Dallas and Beyond (1976, with Paul Hoch and Russell Stetler)
Crime and Cover-Up: The CIA, the Mafia, and the Dallas-Watergate Connection (1977)
The Iran-Contra Connection: Secret Teams and Covert Operations in the Reagan Era
    (1987, with Jonathan Marshall and Jane Hunter)
Coming to Jakarta: A Poem about Terror (1988, 1989, poetry)
Cocaine Politics: Drugs, Armies, and the CIA in Central America
    (1991, 1992, 1998, with Jonathan Marshall)
Listening to the Candle: A Poem on Impulse (1992, poetry)
Deep Politics and the Death of JFK (1993, 1996)
Crossing Borders (1994, poetry)
Oswald, Mexico, and Deep Politics (1994, 2007, 2013)
Drugs, Contras and the CIA: Government Policies and the Cocaine Economy (2000)
Minding the Darkness: A Poem for the Year 2000 (2000, poetry)
Drugs, Oil, and War: The United States in Afghanistan, Colombia, and Indochina
    (2003)
The Road to 9/11: Wealth, Empire, and the Future of America (2007)
The War Conspiracy: JFK, 9/11 and the Deep Politics of War (2008)
Mosaic Orpheus (2009, poetry)
*American War Machine: Deep Politics, the CIA Global Drug Connection, and the Road
    to Afghanistan* (2010)
*Oswald, Mexico, and Deep Politics: Revelations from CIA Records on the Assassination
    of JFK* (1994, 1995, 2013)
Tilting Point (2012, poetry)
The American Deep State: Wall Street, Big Oil, and the Attack on U.S. Democracy
    (2014)
Dallas '63: The First Deep State Revolt Against the White House (2015)

There is more than one way to read my often complex and intertextual poems. I recommend that you begin by reading the poem itself, ideally out loud, and ignore for the moment any sidenotes or references that may accompany it. Whatever you do after that is up to you.

—Peter Dale Scott

CONTENTS

HAIKU

Walking on Darkness

BEFORE READING THIS BOOK

take a morning walk outside
and imagine the white stars
over your head

you are confident are there
because you have seen them
though only at night

and then when your mind has expanded
think of the earth's surface you tread on
curving away to maybe Paris

The next takes a little doing
but when you have the stars and curve in mind
imagine how the space over your head

is mirrored darkly
deep down under your feet
with all last evening's stars

until you feel our planet
surrounded
smaller even than a bit of dust

Bless the Huge Unknown
within us
that can do this

and ask kindness
for those on this crowded mantle
who are suffering

Now you can read
but begin with something very great
perhaps a Song of Innocence by Blake.

CLOUD-RICH

For Karen Croft

At eighty I began to notice clouds
no longer as mere omens, metaphors
or even as bearers of blessed rain
but in themselves: each one in a cloud-rich sky

a creation to be climbed in the mind's eye
as an angel would an Alp, or like an elm
humbling us with its vertical majesty
and so unlike the next majestic elm

Listen to those discords that their leaves
make in the wavering wind, no longer just
a flat susurrus, more a symphony

or symphonic tune-up at a concert
cavernous with echoes and allusions
it could take a lifetime to enjoy

LANGUAGE DEATH

Discomfort on a fog-wet morning
as I walk below
the sycamores muttering
like ghosts of Muwekmas

who once wove waterproof baskets
out of ferns and redbud
singing in Yok-Utian dialects
before my ancestors spoke Erse—

am I now feeling guilt
from that hope in the early sixties
by acquiring freedom of speech
we could *change the world*

in expansion of consciousness
while in the state of California
three hundred dialects
of a hundred languages were dying off   *Frank 153*

much like Jefferson proclaiming
the Indian in body and mind
equal to the white man   *Jefferson 8:186*
while also hoping *to reshape*

Native American societies
to *fit more comfortably within*
his expanding "empire for liberty"   *Bernstein 175*
a naive arrogance limiting

his message of equality
that so inspired Young Europe
yet masked a fatal ignorance
that would founder in the Third World

as the railroads pushed westward
unstorying vast bison habitats
poets forgot the *helmsman's governing hand*   *Whitman 431*
and instead declaimed *This land was ours*   *Frost 316*

then I remembered Laos
a so-called communist country
which still has 86 languages
only two of which are dying   *Ethnologue*

their agriculture of slash and burn
only unsustainable
because the advent of western medicine
has so increased longevity

their women must come south to work
like the one who could not speak Thai
when giving me a gentle massage
in the former kingdom of Nan

and last night I dreamt of a deep lake
in the Little Saguenay Fish and Game Club
where experienced Abenaki hands
tied a Blue Wing Olive on my childish line

a dream which turned nightmarish
when the lake evaporated
leaving me in a crowded parking lot
and I could not find Ronna at the ATM

that fantasy that one could redirect
the dominant power of the world
with *A Citizen's White Paper on Vietnam*   *Schurmann*
is also over

yet part of me still wants
to solve America
a potsherd with exquisite markings
prised from the black loam of an October field

a sunken birchbark canoe
still rosin-sealed and sewn with spruce root
an unfinished arrowhead
in the glinty flakes beside the grinding stone

or a Muwekma song *Ten Coyotes*
sung on a wax cylinder
by the great-grandfather
of a respiratory therapist in Turlock—   *Tremain*

all relics!—like this poem I dedicate
to the last of my Scott cousins
who still remain in Quebec
and whose mother tongue is French.

BIBLIOGRAPHY

Bernstein, R.B. *Thomas Jefferson: The Revolution of Ideas*. New York: Oxford University Press, 2004.

Ethnologue: Languages of the World, http://www.ethnologue.com/country/LA/default/***EDITION*** . In Laos 48 non-official un-written languages are vigorous, compared to over 100 in China, and two (Angloromani [Gypsy] and Hutterite German) in the United States.

Frank, L., and Kim Hogeland. *First Families: A Photographic History of California Indians*. Berkeley, CA: Heyday Books, 2007.

Frost, Robert. *The Poetry of Robert Frost*, ed. Edward Connery. Lathem. New York: Holt, Rinehart and Winston, 1969.

Jefferson, Thomas, ed. Julian P. Boyd, Charles T. Cullen, John Catanzariti, Barbara B. Oberg, et al. *Papers*. Princeton: Princeton University Press, 1950-.

New York Times. July 9, 2913. "Egypt Is Arena for Influence of Arab Rivals," http://www.nytimes.com/2013/07/10/world/middleeast/aid-to-egypt-from-saudis-and-emiratis-is-part-of-struggle-with-qatar-for-influence.html?pagewanted=all&_r=0.

Franz Schurmann, Peter Dale Scott, Reginald Zelnik. *The Politics of Escalation in Vietnam*. Boston: Beacon Press, 1966.

Kerry Tremain, "A Faith in Words." *California Monthly*, September 2004, http://web.archive.org/web/20080404221853/www.alumni.berkeley.edu/Alumni/Cal_Monthly/September_2004/A_faith_in_words.asp.

Walt Whitman, ed. Michael Moon. *Leaves of Grass and Other Writings*. New York: W.W. Norton, 1974.

AN OLD MAN OUT AFTER BREAKFAST

For Sylvia Boorstein

Snapdragon shadow on the sidewalk
      a baby in its carriage
    smiling at a giant Great Dane

a half inch inside
      this sycamore I hug
    sap flowing upwards

Be guided from within
      the principal hornist at the Met
    learned from her dharma teacher

after centuries of the blind advice
      to Odysseus in the underworld
    curb your instinct   *Odyssey 11:105*

an overhanging rosebush
      and a jogger so close
    I feel again that power

of the wholly unexpected
      the intricate feathers
    of the barn owl splayed

in glinting broken glass
      at the side of the desert road
    or that smile from the tour guide

under the Thai waterfall
      the spray lighting up her face
    at the maelstrom's edge

in a gorge so deep
      the others were too prudent to climb down
    one moment indefinable

and of no consequence
      the horn player's Schumann fragment
   at Sylvia's anniversary

the light from the meteoric fireball
      on the hill slope of yuccas
   or when sharpening my pencil

I smell those cedars again
      or that elusive ex-student
   wistful perhaps from her mother's early death

who smuggled a whole boatload of marijuana
      with her biker boyfriend
   one kiss by a mountain stream

and she burst into tears
      I thought you were interested
   in my mind. . . .

And so what is this oxymoron
      deluding and sustaining us
   for decades

the meaning of life?

TO MY WIFE RONNA

i

At first I barely noticed
the tall blue and white hydrangea
around the corner

but now having lived nearby
for almost two decades
I look more and more closely

within the large white veined
sepals that surround each head
to their unexplored forest

of tumbled blue florets
each one with symmetrical
tremulable stamens

moving me to say
you
are more beautiful than you know

ii

Though we have said it a thousand times
I will say it again

If a little bird
had visited our first lunch
in the garden at Augusta's

to say *You two*
are going to get married

We would have been out of there
instantly

at top speed

in opposite directions

                    iii
and I will never know
what alien whim persuaded me

when we were still more or less strangers
and could talk to each other so freely

because each of us was involved
with someone else

to phone you long distance
from the Hampstead tube station

and risk saying to you
à propos of nothing at all

I love you

                    iv
So we went on
to dance together

on the moonlit balcony
looking down on Lake Como

on the deck of the Queen Mary
with no land in sight

and on the tour boat in a narrow fjord—
to the crash of a glacier calving

You took me to the Galilean valley
where thousands of cranes from Siberia
darkened the afternoon sun

you arranged a Tasman boat ride
with gannets plunging all around us
and dolphins leaping beside our bow

breakfasts beside the river in Bangkok
where we could almost touch
the endless rafts of water-hyacinths

on the terrace at Portofino
overlooking the fishing boats
under the centuries-old wisteria vine

or facing the Tetons
where in front of our tablecloth
moose and elk grazed together

in the beaver-dammed swamp

v

But all this was superficial
just grazing the earth's mantle

even your introducing me
to the simplicities of Buddhist life

in the rice paddies of northern Thailand
was less important

than your guiding me
into the heartland
of my own being

to be more at ease
with my children

to abandon my cop-out role
as *visitor from another country*

and engage myself
first to you

and then also to life

          vi
The turning point
was when you persuaded me
(where others had failed)

to go on a week-long retreat
Our car headed off to the redwoods
in the Land of Medicine Buddha

its trunk heavy with my books
not one of which got opened
as I basked in the discovery

of the miracle *I can sit!*
I was sixty-something

when you first gave me a glimpse
of what had always been there

inside me

          vii
you taught me to meditate
not just as a Buddhist
but as a Theravadan

a practice so old and simple
it holds to the eight-fold path

without those paradoxes
of *crazy wisdom*

that make it possible for others
to live scandalously

as a form of renunciation

and not *want to correct this world*   *Milosz Second Space 8*

                    viii
It was as if you were behind me
guiding us both effortlessly
in a canoe

down the silent stream
at the center of our lives
I did not know existed

to that early land
where from time to time
a warbler may speak directly

into our heart

            ix   A digression
I searched for poems by poets to their wives
to living wives that is

not dead like Milton's or Montale's
and found nothing from poets like Dante

Wordsworth Rilke
what showed first was Robert Burns:

On peace an' rest my mind was bent,
        And, fool I was! I married. . . .

I myself remember Caitlin
lonely and furious in the Laugharne cottage

15

You Americans will kill my husband
He is used to beer not whisky

Dorothy made it into the Cantos
Some cook, some do not cook,
some things cannot be altered   *Pound Cantos 81/518*

while Eliot wrote of a sullen succuba
the bridegroom smoothed his hair
There was blood upon the bed   *Eliot 383*

                              x
You more than I
have known such traumas and depression
you are skilled with the afflicted

On my morning walk
I send threefold *metta* for you
as for no other person

but when times get difficult
it can become less clear
for whose sake I do it

So know this:
that I also give thanks
with the whole of my being

to whatever force this is
in the tall sycamores
sustaining my life

that you are my life

that you are my wife

                                        June 29, 2012

TAVERN UNDERWORLD

In the UN Diplomatic Bar
    that looked down on a seamy waterfront
  I was introduced to the elegant

Mrs. Norman Holmes Pearson
    known for turning up with young male poets
  in this case Tambimuttu famous

for having published in *Poetry London*
    poets like Treece and Gascoyne
  and my parents' friend Betty Smart

whose book-length lament
    on her scandalous betrayal
  by the married poet George Barker

and their subsequent arrest in Arizona
    was bought up by her social-minded mother
  back in Ottawa and then burned

I shared reminiscences with Tambi
    of fabled London pubs like the Fitzroy
  where someone pointed out *that Sylvia Bitch*

and a ponce assured me that a Mousehole weekend
    had once been proffered him by Eliot
  or my night with the Roberts—MacBryde and Colquhoun—

who went on when really drunk to trash the flat
    of my harmless writer friend Chris Wanklyn
  remembered today because he made it into

the *Letters* of William S. Burroughs
    And precisely because I was so well suited
  for life now in the Diplomatic Lounge

I who'd earlier turned down the chance
      to sit at Pound's feet with S at St. Elizabeths
   was caught up once again

like Dante's Ulysses in that ancient urge
      to seek *experience* where we don't belong *Inf 26:116*
   and entreated Tambi to be my guide *cf. Inf 1.130*

back into that tavern underworld
      peopled with dropouts from the Unreal City
   with its tall skyscrapers of tinted glass

the White Horse in those days
      so crowded with those remembering
   Dylan's death just three years before

we preferred a small bar across the street
      perhaps the one to which Caitlin fled *Caitlin Thomas*
   when pissed off at Dylan once again

after the two of them—in their *furor*
      poeticus – broke objets d'art and *cf. Plato Ion 533d*
overturned tables at a *party in their honor* *Brinnin Dylan 146*

as if to cry out to a stricken world
      as once our prophets did *Not this*
   Assuredly not this

Tambi and I were just witnesses
      in this narrow bar where anything could happen
   when one night we watched four thugs

burst in as a team to beat up their target
      a bespectacled slightly sweaty man
   kicking him mercilessly on the floor

until they drove off
        Tambi and I picked him up
    I carefully restored to his bruised face

his gold-rimmed glasses
        then suddenly the toughs were back
    to beat and kick him again still harder

this time his glasses into his face
        till there was—as I recall—much blood
    what happened next now completely forgotten

above all the *overwhelming question*
        was he, as we first thought, now blind?
    a fact far too important to be remembered

swept up in this wind of useless memories
        Kasper burning S's books by Freud   *Marsh John Kasper 7*
    so infected by Pound's rant about the Jews

he would soon get himself arrested
        as he became a major suspect
    in a string of Southern synagogue bombings—

what is this this paradox that compels
        me to disgorge these conflicted memories
    and yet withhold S's published name?

and what is this deficit in our daily life
        that has driven us since Homer to seek truth
from the darkness of the underworld?   *Odyssey 10:539, 11:96*

the Quebec tavern men's room wall
        where I had scribbled *Daryl is a poet!*
    inspiring beneath it *Is she? Well fuck a snake!*

or those first all-night bouts on the waterfront
  in Montreal with veterans from the war
 who drank as if there was nothing now to learn

or all the useless foreign ships locked
  in the winter ice of the Lachine Canal
 seen by a boy at the top of Westmount Mountain

all now gone

BIBLIOGRAPHY

Brinnin, John. *Dylan Thomas in America*. London: J.M. Dent, 1956.
Marsh, Alec. *John Kasper and Ezra Pound: Saving the Republic*. London: Bloomsbury Academic, 2015.
Smart, Elizabeth. *By Grand Central Station I Sat Down and Wept*. New York: Vintage, 1992.

WILD MAN IN THE BATHROOM MIRROR

Not yet fully awake
I recognize the nightshirt
but not the bleary-eyed

disheveled savage
occupying it
who when I investigate him

responds to my quite
reasonable curiosity
with a series of scowls and contortions

the nerve of him
coming up so close!
who does he think he is?

What a relief
only a few minutes later
to see him become

the polite person known
to me and all my friends
hair properly brushed

his half-smile concealing
all but the easiest
thoughts to get along with

and unmindful of that grizzled
barbarian
inspired by who knows what

still half-remembered primal dreams

APPEARANCES

Issa: This world
        is no bigger than
    a dewdrop world
and yet   and yet

It was the Age of Aquarius
        the 1960s
    when one followed desire

not logic or duty
        Make love not war!
    as I recalled

at 5 a.m. this morning
        the young blonde angel
    in my Dante class

who told me in office hour
        fifty years ago
    she was dropping out of school

to dedicate her life
        to skiing in Squaw Valley
    and gave me a full frontal

erotic farewell hug
        and then asked me
    Why do you do this? meaning

why did I a campus
        anti-Vietnam war speaker
    teach eclogues in Anglo-Latin

about pastoral friendship
        by Saxon-speaking Northumbrian monks
    in the early Middle Ages

living among the ruins
    of Roman cities
      they called *the work of giants*   *enta geweorc*

and I   jolted for a moment
    answered   *I don't know*
      which I now think was not just true

but the right answer for the moment
    I did know for sure that when
      another student in the class

came to tell me
    she had been so persuaded
      by these medieval writings

she was dropping out of school
    to become a Zen nun
      under Baker Roshi in San Francisco

I with some awareness
    of the Zen Center situation
      was stricken with acute self-doubt

but still kept teaching Dante
    who inspired by a mind
      more profound than the mind

of our frontal lobes
    wrote of the need
      to transcend Virgilian reason

as well as erotic passion
    as if looking down
      from the highest heavenly circle

on our tiny world
    and whom I a fugitive
      from Sciences Po   *Institut d'Etudes Politiques*

had first read while hitch-hiking
    in the French Midi
      when every Romanesque church

and Benedictine monastery
    seemed a welcome haven
      from those soulless meetings

of the 1950s
    French Socialist Party
      I had come to Europe to study

and maybe be part of
    All this became so clear
      at 5 am this morning

from the illuminating moment
    at yesterday's small lunch
      of authors a whistle-blower

and founders of webzines
    at the rickety round table
      in our garden courtyard

plotting how to save democracy
    by forcing the release of documents
      still held illegally by the CIA

when suddenly Ajahn Pasanno
    from the Buddhist monastery
      Wat Abhayagiri   *Redwood Valley CA*

eight hours before I expected
        walked in his saffron robes
    with placid measured tread

through the narrow passage
        between our backed-up chairs
    and the datura tree

like one of the heavenly messengers
        who changed the Buddha
    an apparition

as incongruous as a skit
        out of Monty Python
    yet my reaction was to be

acutely embarrassed
        our machinations
    now seemed mere *papañca*

proliferations of the mind
        then at 5 a.m. this morning
    my life suddenly

undivided
        I saw what I had glimpsed
    when twenty-one at Taizé

in a 12th-century windowless
        Burgundian village church
    where the monks observed the offices

even at midday
        with candles to enlighten us
    something beyond

the desires in modern movies
    we have access to
  an alternity

awaiting us
    and already within us
  and I said in response out loud

That's why I did this!
    everything that matters
  is to move us

to another way

July 2, 2014

THE REST OF THIS POEM IS NOT IN WORDS

The crowded train empties a little
and a dozen hands beckon him at eighty-six
to the one free seat

where he sits in front of a young woman
whose face is not unusual but pure
and vacant because she is listening

to music wired up from her lap
The simple curve from eyebrow down to nostril
reminds him distinctly of a Flemish Virgin

while her lashes in their tiny sunbursts catch
the bright inward distance of her eyes. . . .

That night he dreams of seeing a full moon
shrouded in pastels of Rothko blue   such blue

he and the others cry out, "Omigod!"
above the lake so crystalline and bright

you can see the fish in it. . . .

GREEK THEATER

Mario Savio and the Socratic Quest

> But in changing the city's desires instead of complying with them . . .
> that is the only business of a good citizen.
> —Plato, *Gorgias* 517 B-C

It has taken weeks
    of unsettled half-awareness
  for me to recognize

the student wrestled to the ground   *Cohen Freedom's Orator 213*
    by six policemen in uniforms
  a baton menacing his neck

(an arm across his throat
      to keep him from speaking)   *San Francisco Chronicle December 9 1964*
  on the cover of this book

about how J. Edgar Hoover
    slipped lies to the *San Francisco Examiner*
  advancing the career of Ronald Reagan   *Rosenfeld Subversives 212-13, 227*

is Mario Savio   *leader of Berkeley Free Speech Movement*
    on the stage of the Greek Theater   *December 7 1964; Rosenfeld Subversives 224*
  wrecking the well-planned closure

of the assembly called to proclaim
    an end to the protests and sit-ins
  of the Free Speech Movement

and the inauguration
    of a *new era of freedom under law*   *Rosenfeld Subversives 223*
  by an ambitious professor   *Cohen Freedom's Orator 213-14*

hoping thereby to become
    our next Chancellor
  who defended the war on national TV

28

and is now less googled
> than his daughter a language poet   *Leslie Scalapino*
The anticlimax when Mario

came back out only to announce
> there would be a Free Speech rally   *Cohen Freedom's Orator 213-14*
on the Sproul Hall steps   *Rosenfeld Subversives 224*

up-ended my own planned life
> I was just a few yards away
at the same camera angle

one of those who had urged
> the students to trust
the decency of those in power

my head then filled with Anglo-Latin
> verse from the ninth century
why the return of a cuckoo in spring

spoke to the heart
> expressing aspirations of friendship
more deeply than Virgil could   *Scott Alcuin's Versus de Cuculo*

and did more to invent Europe
> at a higher level—
Christianus sum   *I am a Christian*

non possum militare—   *I cannot make war*   *Acta Maximiliani 1.3*
> than the battle stopping the Moors
on the banks of the Loire

two different kinds of power   *Douglass Gandhi and the Unspeakable 25*
> *bia* the power of dominance   *βία violence Arendt 93*
versus *peithein* the power of persuasion   *πείθειν Schell Unconquerable World 218*

the *virtù* of Macchiavelli
    the *founder* of academic
political science

versus the *politiké techné*   *πολιτικῇ τέχνῃ Gorgias 521D*
    of Socrates and Gandhi
    which persuades by the *force of truth*   *Kornfeld 108 Schell 119*

the cop who thanked Howard Zinn
    for his talk to the Police Academy
then pleaded with him desperately

to please leave the antiwar blockade
    before a little later
    battering him with an outsized club   *Ellsberg*

versus Mario inspiring the crowd
    to immobilize the campus police car
    till Jack Weinberg inside it was released   *Cohen Freedom's Orator 98-120*

the power to transcend enmity
    as I had seen in an iconic moment
alone reading Plato's *Gorgias*

in the Ambassador's huge bed
    when I was *chargé d'affaires* in Warsaw—   *stand-in for absent ambassador*
that the way to change the world

was not through international treaties
    but through *changing the city's desires*   *Plato Gorgias 503-21*
the power of persuasion

versus that of the nightstick
    or even the diplomatic service
with all its tempting frills—

the cook the chauffeur   that flag up ahead on the limo
    the estate weekend up the Hudson
    where baffled ducks were released

for the half-drunk guests to shoot
    the sit-down banquet at Schönbrunn   *Vienna Imperial Palace*
    for six hundred people

served by liveried footmen—
    which I willingly abandoned
    so I could teach in a university

the heritage of the *Patrologia Latina*
    which I had skimmed so greedily
    my first semester back

and then Dante   *la mala condotta*   *misguidance*
    è la cagion che'l mondo ha fatto reo   *is why the world goes wrong*
    e non natura che'n voi sia corrotta   *and not your nature that is corrupt*
                          Dante Purgatorio 16:103-05

Well—little could I foresee
    how Mario in an instant
    (who himself had been inspired

by *the plays of Sophocles*
    and Aeschylus and Euripides   *Cohen Freedom's Orator 35*
    before being beaten in Mississippi

for walking in public with a black man
    as part of Freedom Summer)   *Cohen Freedom's Orator 59-60*
    had changed me from a Latinist

into an activist
    no longer a mere spectator
    (as I had been five days earlier

when the students filed into Sproul Hall
    singing *We shall overcome*)
  that same evening I spoke

at the crisis faculty meeting
  and only one month later
my first public appeal

to get troops out of Vietnam
    which though I could not know it
  would soon bring a painful end

to my evenings with Milosz
    debating the right English
  for *what is poetry*

that does not save
    nations or peoples?
  a heartbreaking loss at the time

but not one that deterred me
    as much as the crazy violence
  that developed after Mario

moved away from leadership
  not wanting the Movement
    to become too dependent on him

in the dramatic struggle between
  two kinds of decency
one struggling for an end

to racial hiring
    in the local supermarkets
  one that of the U.S. middle class

who did not want their kids dropping acid
    or cursing *Amerikkka*
  and so when given a chance

December 2 1964; Rosenfeld 216-22
Scott Charlie Sellers 1

Cohen Freedom's Orator 214-15

Milosz New Collected Poems 78
Haven An Invisible Rope 69

Cohen Freedom's Orator 253

Cohen Freedom's Orator 237-38

Rosenfeld Subversives 176-77

Ruether America Amerikkka

32

voted for Ronald Reagan
>   *the great persuader*   *Broder Washington Post 6/7/04*
while Richard Aoki

as a paid FBI informant
>   armed the Black Panthers   *Rosenfeld Subversives 418-19, 421*
But Mario returned in the 1980s

and revived a dormant campus
>   *changing the city's desires*   *Plato Gorgias 517 B-C*
with his *use of philosophy*

Socrates and Thoreau   *Cohen Freedom's Orator 202*
>   when he spoke of shifting *our values*
for an America *less dominated*

by production for war
>   and more *by human needs*   *Cohen Freedom's Orator 280, 348*
inspiring—yes!—even faculty like myself

to monitor a divestment protest
>   in support of the South African resistance   *Rosenfeld Subversives 501*
with white armbands torn from a sheet in our basement

all helping to stoke *a nationwide demonstration*   *15 ARRESTED New York Times 4/17/85*
>   till finally the UC Regents
divested $3 billion in funds   *Skelton Los Angeles Times 12/11/13*

so that—I do believe—
>   Mario helped contribute
to the liberation of South Africa

Mandela himself credited California
>   *with helping push his* country
>   *toward racial integration*   *Skelton Los Angeles Times 12/11/13*

Truth-force as history!   Oh John Searle   *Satyagraha*
>   you recognized in your student Mario's speeches
a kind of freshness combined

with *a certain deep intellectual vision*   *Cohen Freedom's Orator 189*
    but when you later came to see the movement
    as a bunch of *losers*   *Cohen Freedom's Orator 317*

with *unreasonable expectations*   *Searle Interview 5*
    you were resuming your distinguished career
    as an academic philosopher

while it was Mario
    at what you called a *second-rate* university   *Cohen Freedom's Orator 316*
  who remained on the *straight path*

of the Socratic quest
    to change by persuasion
  our misguided world

curbing the authority of *violence*
    by appealing to those hints of freedom
  encoded in our DNA

that truth-force enabling a movement
    to overcome as Mario said
  a *machine so odious*

you've got to make it stop   *Cohen Freedom's Orator 183, 458-59*

BIBLIOGRAPHY

Acta Maximiliani, ed. H. Musurillo. *The Acts of the Christian Martyrs*. Oxford: Clarendon Press, 1972.

Arendt, Hannah. *Between Past and Future: Eight Exercises in Political Thought*. New York: Penguin Books, 1993.

Broder, David S. "The Great Persuader." *Washington Post*, June 7, 2004. http://www.washingtonpost.com/wp-dyn/articles/A21076-2004Jun6.html.

Cohen, Robert. *Freedom's Orator: Mario Savio and the Radical Legacy of the 1960s*. New York: Oxford University Press, 2009.

Douglass, James W. *Gandhi and the Unspeakable: His Final Experiment with Truth*. Maryknoll, NY: Orbis Books, 2012.

Ellsberg, Daniel. "A Memory of Howard Zinn." AntiWar.com, January 27, 2010. http://antiwar.com/blog/2010/01/27/a-memory-of-howard-zinn/.

Gleason, Ralph J. "The Tragedy at The Greek Theater." *San Francisco Chronicle*, December 9, 1964. http://www.fsm-a.org/stacks/R_ Gleason.html.

Haven, Cynthia, ed. *An Invisible Rope: Portraits of Czeslaw Milosz.* Athens: Ohio University Press, 2011. Contains Peter Dale Scott, "A Difficult, Inspirational Giant."

New York Times, April 17, 1985. http://www.nytimes.com/1985/04/17/ us/15-arrestedon-berkeley-campus-in-protest-on-south-africa-policy.html.

Rosenfeld, Seth. *Subversives: The FBI's War on Student Radicals, and Reagan's Rise to Power.* New York: Farrar, Straus and Giroux, 2012.

Ruether, Rosemary Radford. *America, Amerikkka: Elect Nation and Imperial Violence.* Oakville, CT: Equinox, 2007.

Schell, Jonathan. *The Unconquerable World: Power, Nonviolence, and the Will of the People.* New York: Metropolitan Books, 2003.

Scott, Peter Dale. "Alcuin's Versus de Cuculo: The Vision of Pastoral Friendship." *Studies in Philology*, 62 no. 4 (July 1965), 510–30. http://www.enotes.com/alcuin-essays/alcuin/peter-dale-scott-essay-date-july-1965.

Scott, Peter Dale. "Charlie Sellers at Berkeley." A Tribute at the Charles G. Sellers 90th Birthday Symposium, Berkeley, CA, September 7, 2013. http://nature.berkeley.edu/~c-merchant/Sellers/tributes/1.pdf.

John Searle Interview. Conversations with History, Institute of International Studies, University of California, Berkeley. http://globetrotter.berkeley.edu/people/Searle/searle-con5.html.

Skelton, George. "Leading the Way to Justice in South Africa." *Los Angeles Times*, December 11, 2013. http://articles.latimes.com/2013/dec/11/local/ la-me-cap-mandela-20131212.

DONNA OSCURA

Cara beltà che amore
Lunge m'inspiri o nascondendo il viso,
Fuor se nel sonno il core

Ombra diva mi scuoti,
O ne' campi ove splenda
Più vago il giorno e di natura il riso . . .

(Beloved beauty who inspires
love from afar, your face concealed
except when your celestial image
stirs my heart in sleep, or in the fields
where light and nature's laughter
shine more lovely . . .)
                    —Leopardi, Alla Sua Donna

"As you must know, there was much material about your father in Sandra
Djwa's book about P.K. Page. It must be odd for you to read, but your father
came across as a very sympathetic figure, I thought."
                    —Tracy Ware

A glimpse last night . . .
          a smile . . .
     a laugh that was my own heart laughing . . .

I had not seen you for decades
          after my first solitary miserable
     experiences of adulthood

when I would sing of you
          down vineyard lanes
     in a country and a language not my own

Te viatrice in questo arido suolo
          Io mi pensai. Ma non è cosa in terra
     Che ti somigli

(I imagined you a fellow voyager
          on this arid soil. But there is nothing on earth
     that resembles you)
                    Leopardi Alla Sua Donna

36

too much in love
          with this scrap of Leopardi
     to deal with the Albertan in Paris

who practiced Poulenc each morning
          for some international competition
     on the basement piano

in the Maison Canadienne
          even though I had been assured
     she had a crush on me

Now for decades I have not missed you
          except when I open my mind
     for a few minutes each morning

to the purely imaginable
          when you never come
     desire reaching out to empty space

not wasted, since what has enforced
          your absence was my revisiting
     those very same vineyard lanes

on my first honeymoon with Maylie
          and now more recently my first
     sustainable happy marriage

So why now? yes, I have an urgent deadline
          that's when poems come, but never you
     It must have been TV last night

the moment of Roosevelt's death
          when Eleanor coming to retrieve the body
     learned that the woman with him when he died

was the woman who thirty years before
        had broken their marriage, or, no,
    not broken it completely, but reduced it

to something merely practical and useful
        leaving him free to romance the world
    with an intriguing smile, masking great pain

and yet cheerful enough to save
        if not his wife and himself
    at least the country from depression

He was in thrall to Power
        even though, to those who deal with her up close
    she is a Unkempt Whore, *una puttana sciolta*   *Purg 32:149*

but why am I talking Roosevelt
        and why I am glad
    neurosis made him a great President

who got factories to reopen
        put millions back to work
    the best crisis leaders it is said

are always *mentally ill*
        or mentally abnormal   *Ghaemi A First-Rate Madness 17*
when all this (as I only realize

weeks after last night's visit)
        is not really about FDR
    but about FRS—my father

in his own time of pain
        that silent dinner
    when he finally said to my mother

he had *night work at the office*
  and I still an undergraduate
took the bus down to McGill

and confirmed his window was dark
  A big deal? can a darkened window
affect a whole life? I think of you

cara beltà, and of my lifelong
  inquiries of monks
and of that woman whose talk

in the darkness of her dingy basement flat
  turned to what I thought untimely
allusions to another man

and now there is a whole book
  about a well-known poet
in which her *scandalous romance*

with my father *takes centre stage*   *Ball Winnipeg Free Press*
  and a book to come surely
about the artist Paterson Ewen

who suffered breakdown and electroshock
  after his wife foolishly believed
my father would marry her   *Graham Canadian Art Fall 1996*

And as for my father   Well
  he had a public heart
and did much for Canadian civil rights

winning *2 landmark legal cases*
  before the Supreme Court   *Canadian Encyclopedia*
and the truth is I too loved him

not just for having shared
      his brilliant conversation
   but also to have learned

from his skill and patience
      how to make a campfire with wet wood
   by shaving twigs when there was no birch bark

the inner heart as I have written
      of that public man   *Scott Minding the Darkness 79*
   and not least his faith that became mine

in a cosmic order tending towards peace
      So have I accepted he was not perfect?
   and does this explain my own obsession

with the imperfections of the Unkempt Lady?
      and is this why you
   cara donna di beltà

when you came back last night
      in the darkness a second time
   jocund with energy

it was to say good-bye
      as if confirming
   that the two of us

so intimate in my youthful pain
were now not for each other?

                       September 21, 2014

NOTES

Ball, Jonathan. "First Biography of P.K. Page Suffers With Style Issues." *Winnipeg Free Press*, November 3, 2012. http://www.winnipegfreepress.com/arts-and-life/entertainment/books/first-biography-of-pk-page-suffers-with-style-issues-177072291.html.

Canadian Encyclopedia. http://www.thecanadianencyclopedia.ca/en/article/frank-scott/.

Ghaemi, Nassir. *A First-Rate Madness: Uncovering the Links between Leadership and Mental Illness.* New York: Penguin Press, 2011.

Graham, Ron. "Paterson Ewen: The Artist's Dilemma." *Canadian Art,* Fall 1996, 70-79. http://canadianart.ca/features/1996/09/01/paterson-ewen-the-artists-dilemma/.

Scott, Peter Dale. *Minding the Darkness: A Poem for the Year 2000.* New York: New Directions, 2000.

FINCHITY

These finches that flock to the openings
of my squirrel-proof steel birdfeeder
that stands in our courtyard
are like my thoughts

their gold now lusterless
in this late season no longer
resplendent in the dawn

they fly in and out
before my wide-open eyes
that should by intention be shut

till thoughts become finches
and finches thoughts

Between the cavern
of all I might have become

and this clutch
of pure finchity

what refuge
from these faint stirrings of the heart?

BREAKFAST WINDOW

For Carol and Walter Beebe, Nanette Schorr and Ralph White

Nursing his breakfast special
under the vintage tin ceiling
of the Village Den

with no newspaper to read
he watches the pageant
of New Yorkers hurrying

blondes in fashionable boots
emerging fresh-faced from the heavy
weight-lifting contraptions in the spa

businessmen with briefcases
brushing past the homeless
and the bassist trundling his double bass

the children and their matching parents
all of them headed in the same direction
ambling at first and then running

except for the identical twins
on identical pink trikes
with identical pink baskets

Can he really have been all these ages?
He sees how his mind has been letting go
of its cherished baggage

from the indefinable angst
of that awkward hand-drawn fifth-grade valentine
or that blind date dinner with his first wife

to the trill of the winter wren
that lifted him to some sort of threshold
in the Land of Medicine Buddha

He sees he is already
spilling slowly outwards
like the pierced yolk of this over-easy egg

the scattered remnants
from last night's irretrievable dream

West Village, New York City, March 16, 2010

CHAINSAW DHAMMA

After the pre-dawn hour of chanting
and meditation in the dhamma hall
on *Setting in Motion the Wheel of Dhamma*
lokutaro yo ca tadattha-dipano
(that which is beyond the conditioned world)

and after the hot oatmeal
prepared by the *anagarikas* in white   *lay attendants*
remains of frost dripping off the kitchen roof

the monks in saffron robes
reassemble for the morning meeting
the chores monk assigns a team
to cut away all the brushwood on the trail
below a height of thirteen feet
so that the Nor-Cal cement truck
can drive securely up to the unfinished
Monks' Utilities Building
without scratching its paint

He warns to be mindful
when using the chainsaw
to cut no more than
two or three manzanitas in a row
the wood is so hard
the chainsaw will heat up
stretch
and maybe snake off its
saw bar rail

Anicca vata sankhara
(all forms are impermanent)

Pali words
that have been chanted daily
without a break

for over two thousand years

Wat Abhayagiri, January 10, 2009

45

A PRAYER FOR MY GRANDDAUGHTER

For Marianna

Yeats in his tower battered by sea winds
Studied his cradled daughter with great gloom.
No longer buoyed by earlier hopes that art
Could calm a tormented nation's frenzied heart,
All argument futile now, when war
Brought ragged soldiers to his very door,
He prayed she grow to be of a different mind,
Freed from the hatreds still surrounding him.

Four decades later my Zen Buddhist wife
At our children's births, when fixed bayonets
Lined our own streets, repeated Yeats's prayer
That a child be spared the fury of the strife
shared by both sheriffs and the militants,
Recover the soul's radical innocence
And establish concord in a house
Graced by custom and by ceremony.

Thus surely grounded, our children chose,
Not caring for the way this country tends,
To leave their university careers:
Cassie to live and work among the poor
My sons to earn a living as musicians,
While John, your father, to our surprise,
The first in the family not to be baptized
By us, led services at church for years.

Thus you, Marianna, have been provided
With a glimpse of worlds beyond experience.
While all around you others not so guided
Are listless from undefined identity.
Your house returns to custom: Latin grace
At meals, home schooling, music, no TV,
Hamsters, psalms, ballet, the whimsical chance
To dress like Alice in a Victorian dress.

Those wavelets on our bay are never wild,
Our wars are fought on distant continents.
Yet you, however well protected, fled
A clod on the trail you feared was a dead bird
While gulls flew in towards us to be fed.
I pray that you, now ten, will draw on faith
To be equanimous when facing death,
Know when to withdraw, when not to be deterred.

I wish that I could guarantee a world
Where kindness is requited, as were best.
But now for a half century or more
This country has continued to make war,
Reaping war's harvest: hatred, drugs and crime.
May you still learn which instincts to obey
Until it is painful to have inflicted pain
And generosity makes you happiest.

May you be different from those who seek
Authenticity in what's unique,
Dismissing the commonplace as mere cliché.
Be prompted by your own simplicity
So that you will be rooted like a tree
Nourished by living water, yielding fruit,
Whose leaves will not be torn by blustering gales
Nor wither from the drought of rootless thought.

Be rooted, not too rooted. Reach like Yeats
Up out from nature into artifice.
Master your steps of classical ballet
Contorting natural impulse into grace
With the refined mastery of those before you
Till you are moved by such intuition
Music itself will guide you in the dance
to w*here is no memory and no anticipation.*   *Auden "Ballet's Present*

Eden"

47

TASTING AND SEEING

("to act by not acting, to know by not knowing" —Taoist proverb)

Last night, in *shul*, as we sang *L'kha dodi*
to greet the bride Shabbat, we all turned,
before the last stanza, to the door behind us
and welcomed in a presence not ourselves,
the *Shekinah*, entering to be wed.   *divine presence*
I too, not really Jewish, sensed this change,
the mystic entrance of the unseen bride
Shabbat, the queen of peace and future peace.

And this morning, in church, we sing and turn again
to look behind us, for the arrival
(*"Burst into song, you mountains and your trees"*)   *Isaiah 44:23*
of eight-year-old queens in white with coronets,
boys in white ties, and you, my grandson Peter,
about to be enhanced by your first taste
of paschal wafer and consecrated wine—
your entrance also stirs the rest of us.

My knees, once more as they now so rarely are
on a prayer bench, are no longer quaking
as they did decades ago, out of passionate
uncertainty and doubt, when I, in France,
still a lapsed socialist, was brought by chance
to Taizé's little commune of twelve monks,
and, reading Gilson and Emile Mâle,   *French medievalists*
first glimpsed the future hidden in our past.

Now I feel more secure, next to the knees
of my whole family, all of you—more than I,
this firm bench seems to tell me—all secure
(as my own parents were in unbelief—
The future of man was my father's heaven),
confirmed by the weekly rituals you share
from dress, prayer, and the words of grace
we say each meal before we dine together,

recited for centuries, like *L'kha dodi,*
and, I imagine, likely to survive
this present age of zealots and crusaders
waging war until they all are gone,
leaving behind as residues such faiths
as this one, with a creed that stayed alive,
enforced through time by conquering emperors—
this faith with which you, Peter, will commune.

Here in this church, blacks, Filipinos,
Chinese, Mexicans now line up to sing
O taste and see that the Lord is good,   *Psalm 34:8*
the Thirty-fourth Psalm — *O contemplate*
in my Stone edition of the Hebrew Bible,
but in traditional Christian English, *taste*
(טַעַם—*taam—of Sapience no small part,*   *Paradise Lost 9:1018*
as Adam said, to justify his fall).   *cf. Exodus 16:31, 1 Sam 25:33*

Not really Catholic, I still confess
I love the mass, though somewhat in the way
I was awed by the carvings of Angkor Wat,
or the mystic stones at Carnac, still more
the prostrate hundred thousands at Czestochowa,
or those in the northern Thailand Buddhist wat,   *temple*
where I, like the Thais around me, clutched my string
conveying *metta* from the monks up front,   *loving-kindness*

always a witness to others' certain faith
confirming my own faith in the uncertain
and these families who came to America,
just as Merton and Rabbi Heschel came
from Europe's collapse to Winthrop's commonwealth,
or the Safed *rebbe* in flight from Greece   *Shlomo Alkabetz*
who wrote that the Kabbala bride of peace, Shabbat,
foretells *the city rebuilt on her hill.*   *L'kha dodi 26; cf. Isaiah 44:28*

49

It is hot outside. As we go off to lunch,
Peter's tie is gone. Again he wears
an open shirt and Star Wars baseball cap,
back in this world where changes rarely change,
and again himself. Yet more than his old self—
a communicant (since earthly cities fail)
with a mystery beyond this daily life
which has been tasted and which has been seen.

*   *   *

After the burnings and forced conversions,
The crusaders forcing others to be free,
Amazing grace, if we confront disaster,
Stricken as Paul Celan was, are we wrong
To sing again in praise, kumi uri   קוּמִי אוֹרִי *Celan 314 L'kha dodi 23*
"Stant up"? *The heart has always had its reasons,*   Is
                                                      60:1 tr. Meister Eckhart
Sometimes profound, sometimes in grisly error
Whose violence is undeterred by prayer;
But what of the mysteries of peace we taste in song?

Alameda, California, May 4, 2013

Celan, Paul. *Breathturn into Timestead: The Collected Later Poetry: A Bilingual Edition.* New York: Farrar, Straus and Giroux, 2014.

ANOTHER ROAD

A troubled dream
that the road we are traveling
is temporarily blocked

because—they are saying—
of the bad traffic up ahead
and it is true   we can see

the traffic equally stalled
in front as well as behind the barrier
but look! to the left

of the familiar highway
through the French-speaking village
past the church with its battle-scarred façade

a garden forest
with another road—clean black asphalt—through it
no cars at all

Would I dare take it   I wonder
having no clear idea
where the new route will take us

What if we had to leave our car
amid other cars all like it
heavy with so much needless baggage

though the beginning looks like a park
might there not be rattlesnakes
perhaps even grizzlies?

and what about the risk
that there is no road there at all
only an illusion

of the type that appears in deserts
despite the abundant testimony
of so many poets who have seen it

      *   *   *

Kung and Eleusis
Tao and Aristotle
my father after his life

of constitutional law
attacked by a *tyger*
at the foot of his bed

and after years of sleeping out
from Wales to Styria
a treaty conference in the Vienna Hofburg

to consolidate a diplomatic fabric
that now for a half century
has seemed to be falling apart

to Jerry Rubin and me
at the Vietnam Day Committee
I arguing that the truth

would persuade Congress
to end this crazy war
while Rubin made the case

for rock bands and psychedelics
to reach a mass audience
the year our faculty journal

to speak truth to power
was engulfed by the *Berkeley Barb*
financed by porn ads

with its photos of naked women
and now I see clearly
that Jerry was right

and I was probably wrong

     * * *

And now Chris Hedges
censured by the *New York Times*
for having warned against the folly

of the Iraq War[1]
who once believed
The fantasy of popular revolts

breaking the hegemony of the corporate state
is just that, a fantasy
then unlike me

made the spiritual decision
quoting Tillich
Institutions are always

inherently demonic,
including the Church
to camp out in Zuccotti Park

even though as you admitted
numerous street people
with mental impairment and addictions

tore apart the community
as you must have predicted
No matter! You saw this

---

1   Chris Hedges, "A Father's Gift," *The Dallas Morning News*, June 17, 2006.

as *the trajectory of all movements*
a *kind of dress rehearsal.*
even though you saw *nothing*

that indicates we're preparing
to make that change . . . [2]

2   Bill Moyers, Moyers & Company, Interview with Chris Hedges, July 24, 2012,
http://truth-out.org/news/item/10494-journalist-chris-hedges-on-capitalisms-sacrifice-zones-communi-
ties-destroyed-for-profit#.UBAGSWjGv0w.facebook.

THE ROAD TO DEATH VALLEY FROM LONE PINE

For Jennifer Howard and Tony Cascardi

This time, you wrote the marriage vows yourselves
To care for each other's children, smell the flowers,
Take perspective, give perspective—yes!
love without that hot erotic blindness!

Above all, *Translate love into kindness!*—
The wider horizons of a second marriage,
with youthful Eros transferred into offspring,
open novel space for exploration.

Like the road to Death Valley from Lone Pine
down a desert gulch where folks before you
have blasted the narrows with dynamite

just enough to let a four-wheel through
to wander freely in the open desert
that will blossom like a hothouse after rain.

TRANSLATIONS

DU FU: SPRING VISTA

春望

The kingdom is wrecked, mountains and streams endure,
This spring grass grows deep in the ruined fort.
Feeling the season, flowers evoke tears,
Pain that birds are leaving scares the heart.
War's beacon fires have burned now for three months,
A letter from home costs thousands in gold.
I worry my white hair until it thins,
Soon it will no longer hold a cap-pin.

Original	Pinyin
國破山河在	guó pò shān hé zài
城春草木深	chéng chūn cǎo mù shēn
感時花濺淚	gǎn shí huā jiàn lèi,
恨別鳥驚心	hèn bié niǎo jīng xīn
烽火連三月	fēng huǒ lián sān yuè
家書抵萬金	jiā shū dǐ wàn jīn
白頭搔更短	bái tóu sāo gèng duǎn
渾欲不勝簪	hún yù bù shèng[3] zān

state	broken	mountain	river	remain
city	spring	grass	tree	deep
feel	time	flower	splash	tears
hate	separate	birds	alarm	heart
beacon	fires	endure	three	months
home	letter	cost	10,000	gold
white	head	scratch	even	less
whole	soon	not	equal to hatpin	

3   Mathews (#5754) says that with this meaning *sheng* is in first tone.

DU FU: AUTUMN MEDITATION

秋 兴 八 首 (一)

Jade-hued dew chills the withered maples,
In Wu mountain gorge the air is dreary.
River waves surge against the sky,
Above the pass clouds earth merge in darkness.

Chrysanthemum bushes weep for other days,
One lonely boat links to my home-sick heart.
Quickly get out and tailor winter clothing,
Below Baidi in the dusk they scrub with stones.

玉　　露　　凋　　仿　　枫　　树　　林
yu2　lu2　diao　shang1 feng1 shu4　lin2
Jade　dew　wither　wound maple tree　forest

巫　　山　　巫　　峡　　气　　萧　　森
wu1　shan1　wu1　xia2　qi4　xiao1　sen3
Wu mountain wu　gorge　air desolate dreary

江　　間　　波　　浪　　兼　　天　　涌
jiāng　jiān　bō　làng　jiān　tiān　yǒng
River　on　wave　meet　connect sky　surge

塞　　上　　风　　云　　接　　地　　阴
sài　shàng　fēng　yún　jiē　dì　yīn
Pass　on　wind　cloud　join　earth　dark

从	菊	两	开	他	日	泪
cóng	jú	liǎng	kāi	tā	rì	lèi
Shrub	mum	two	open	other	day	tear

孤	舟	一	系	故	园	心
gū	zhōu	yí	xì	gù	yuán	xīn
Single	boat	one	link	home	town	heart

寒	衣	处	处	催	刀	尺
hán	yī	chù	chù	cuī	dāo	chǐ
Cold	clothes	everywhere		urge	knife	measure

白	帝	城	高	急	暮	砧
bái	dì	chéng	gāo	jí	mù	zhēn
Bai	di	cheng	high	urgent	evening	anvil

ALBRECHT HAUSHOFER: GUILT

I count for little what the Special Court
will name my guilt: my plot and its concern.
I would have been a criminal, if I'd not
always plotted for the Nation's Dawn.
Yes! I am guilty, but not the way you think:
I should have answered sooner duty's call,
more harshly named as evil what was evil—
for far too long I kept my judgment sealed. . . .
In my own conscience is my indicting:
I betrayed for far too long my own awareness,
having lied to myself as I did to others.
Quite early on I saw disaster looming—
I warned—but never loud and clear enough!
Today I know what I was guilty of. . . .

SCHULD

Ich trage leicht an dem, was das Gericht
mir Schuld benennen wird: an Plan und Sorgen.
Verbrecher wär´ ich, hätt´ ich für das Morgen
des Volkes nicht geplant aus eigner Pflicht.
Doch schuldig bin ich anders, als ihr denkt,
ich musste früher meine Pflicht erkennen,
ich muss schärfer Unheil Unheil nennen—
mein Urteil hab ich viel zu lang gelenkt . . .
Ich klage mich in meinem Herzen an:
Ich habe mein Gewissen lang betrogen,
ich hab´ mich selbst und andere belogen.
Ich kannte früh des Jammers ganze Bahn—
Ich hab´ gewarnt—nicht hart genug und klar!
Und heute weiß ich, was ich schuldig war . . .
[Albrecht Haushofer, Sonnet 39, "Guilt"]

Albrecht Haushofer was a member of the so-called Kreisau Circle, a group including aristocrats and clergy who secretly plotted ways to return Germany from Nazi dictatorship to its traditional constitutional past. Because some members were involved in the 1944 plot to kill Hitler, Haushofer and others were arrested, imprisoned, and finally shot just before the war ended.

Although not normally a poet, Haushofer wrote a series of eighty "Moabit Sonnets" in Berlin-Moabit Prison. One of them in particular, "Schuld" ("Guilt" or "Debt"), was in Haushofer's pocket when he was shot; and it has since attracted international attention as a statement of principled resistance to immoral authority. It was brought to my attention by my friend Daniel Ellsberg, who himself faced long imprisonment for his decision to release the Pentagon Papers.

ZBIGNIEW HERBERT: PEBBLE

Here is the translation of Zbigniew Herbert's famous poem "Kamyk," as Czeslaw Milosz and I first published it in 1968:

the pebble
is a perfect creature
equal to itself
mindful of its limits
filled exactly
with a pebbly meaning
with a scent that does not remind one of anything
does not frighten anything away does not arouse desire
its ardour and coldness
are just and full of dignity
I feel a heavy remorse
when I hold it in my hand
and its noble body
is permeated by false warmth
—-Pebbles cannot be tamed
to the end they will look at us
with a calm and very clear eye

Herbert's poem "Pebble" is rightly one of his best known in translation. It was also one of the easiest Herbert poems for Milosz and me to translate, because of its matter-of-fact lucid exposition of a trope that, for the most part, is not dependent on subtleties of language. In essence it is an intellectual warning against the falsity of pathetic fallacies. His emphasis on what has been called "the thingness of things" reminds us of the work of earlier objectivist poets, notably Rilke, Williams, and Ponge.

"Pebble"'s astringent anti-romanticism can be read as a rebuttal to Milosz's early poem 'Love':

. . . whoever sees that way [with love] heals his heart,
Without knowing it, from various ills—
A bird and a tree say to him: Friend. . . .
He doesn't serve the best who understands.

(The sense of a dialogue between poets becomes even stronger when we read the later "Conversation With a Stone" by Wislawa Szymborska: "I knock at the stone's front door./ "It's only me, let me come in."/ "I don't have a door," says the stone.")

Straightforward though the poem may be, it was one of the very few Herbert poems which, precisely because of its tight austerity, gave rise to two irresoluble disagreements between Milosz and myself as to how to translate it. I failed forty years ago to persuade Milosz to accept these two changes. At the time I was filled with awe and gratitude for the exciting and educational experience of translating with him, so I deferred. Nevertheless my two suggested alternatives have since continued to haunt me. How important these nuanced differences are, the reader can judge.

In the first couplet, "kamyk jest stworzeniem/ doskonałym," there is, as is normal in Polish, no article, either definite or indefinite. English requires one, unless you cheat and use a plural—"pebbles"—which would not work well with what follows. I wanted very much to start off in a low key, "a pebble/ is a perfect creature." Milosz, I'm not sure why, insisted on 'the pebble/ is a perfect creature,' establishing a tone which I considered unsuitably elevated, declamatory and didactic. (A definite article is available in Polish, but Herbert chose not to use it, which is a further reason to think of 'a pebble' as the default translation.)

A more serious disagreement arose over the last line. Milosz insisted on translating the last two lines as "to the end they will look at us/ with a calm and very clear eye." I have always believed that we should have followed Herbert's carefully selected word order in Polish (okiem spokojnym bardzo jasnym), which is "[with an] eye calm [and] very clear." In general we agreed that it was important to respect Herbert's very precise choice of word order; but here I think that Milosz followed his own personal preference for a continuous vernacular style, over the slightly heightened resonance of Herbert's final word "clear."

I still disagree with this choice. I find it jarring, as well as metrically awkward, to come down heavily at the end on the false metaphor, "eye;" I believe that Herbert intended the line to proceed from that small metaphor outwards, to the open-ended clarity that characterizes not just the word but the entire poem.

My admiration of Milosz still generates in me the desire to dispute with him. As to which is the better version of "Pebble," I will let the reader decide. Here is mine:

PEBBLE

a pebble
is a perfect creature
equal to itself
mindful of its limits
filled exactly
with a pebbly meaning
with a scent that does not remind one of anything
does not frighten anything away does not arouse desire
its ardor and coldness
are just and full of dignity
I feel a heavy remorse
when I hold it in my hand
and its noble body
is permeated by false warmth
—-Pebbles cannot be tamed
to the end they will look at us
with an eye calm and very clear

THE SPACE BETWEEN
or, Why I Love My *Mathews' Chinese-English Dictionary*

[bracketed characters are not voiced]

You have to see this poem, not just read it aloud
It is not just expressed in sounds
like skyscraper *or perhaps better*
gratte-ciel, *the sky being scratched*

No! In Chinese meanings
are *seen* in ideograms
like the complex word *autumn*   *[perhaps from Etruscan]*

in Chinese 秋 *ch'iu1*

where 火 *huo3—fire*

is applied to 禾 *ho2—ricefields*

for the season when peasants
burn off the stubble
preparing for the next crop

and smoke hangs low
in the flat valleys
between the rocky hills

And 愁 *ch'ou2* meaning *sadness*

(more wistful than 悶 *men4—sadness—*

the *heart* [心*hsin1*] enclosed in a *gate* [門 *men2*]—

meaning also *airtight*)   *Mathews 621*

is written 愁*ch'ou2—*the heart [心*hsin1*]

clouded by burning fields [秋 *ch'iu1*]

64

Now consider the word 間 [*chien1*]
to divide or *separate*
where a *gate* [門 *men2*] encloses

not the *heart* [悶 *men4*]—*sadness*
or a *moon* [閒 *hsien2*]—*leisure*
but the *sun* 日 [*jih4*]

and is different from 析 [*hsi1*]
(*axes* [斤*chin1*] applied to wood [木 *mu4*])
which is also *to divide* or *separate*

but as in *discriminate explain*   *Mathews 366*
whereas 間 *chien1* the sun in the doorway—
the word I once used to describe

my separation from Maylie   *Listening to the Candle 160*
is more open and three-dimensional
the space between

to blame (as we did when married)
intermittent
a division of a house

to part friends   *Mathews 114*

65

GOOGLING FOR NORBERT

At our diplomatic cocktail party
        our first guest was Norbert Ogiński
    the young Polish Count

whose family before the war
        he himself told me
    had four palaces in Warsaw

no beds for the servants
        so that maids slept on the floor
    next to the stove

Norbert was followed
        in a few seconds
    by Mieczysław Rakowski

the editor of *Polityka*
        the communist journal for intellectuals
    who thirty years later

would be *the second-to-last*
        communist Prime Minister of Poland   *Wikipedia,*
                                            "Mieczysław Rakowski"
    For the next half hour

Maylie and I stood at the door
        receiving our guests—forty Poles
    in the fifteen minutes

before the first diplomats arrived
        too late to help separate
    the Count from the Communist

now jammed by the pressure of arrivals
        into the small space behind our sofa
    they shared with a standing lamp.

No matter! I heard afterwards
　　　how grateful Norbert was to meet
　　for the first time since the War

a member of the ruling party
　　　who could help him with needed perks
　　like getting into university

while Rakowski was grateful in turn
　　　to meet his first aristocrat
　　who may have helped him become

(something he was certainly not yet
　　　when I knew him in '59)
　　a charming, multilingual bon vivant　　　*Time 1/25/1982*

whose *reforms* as Prime Minister
　　　came too late and were too little　　*Wikipedia, "Solidarity"*
　　to stave off Solidarity.

Of young Count Norbert
　　　and his four former palaces
　　Google records no trace whatever

except of his family tree:　　　*http://oginski.iatp.by/images/tree.jpg*
　　　the Ogińskis allegedly
　　descended from Rurik

the first Prince of the Rus　　　*d. 879*
　　　owned seventeen estates
　　in Belarus, Lithuania, Poland and Russia　　*http://oginski.*
　　　　　　　　　　　　　　　　　　　　　　　　　iatp.by/ENG/tree.htm

and his ancestor Michal
　　　who died in exile
　　created his own division of cavalry

67

for the Kościuszko Insurrection
as well as an opera
called *Bonaparte au Caire*

and a still-popular Polonaise
you can listen to on the Web

Berkeley May 2006

BERKELEY OAKS

This poem was written when the University was threatening in 2006 to cut down a grove of live oaks, in order to expand its football stadium. Some radical ecologists had responded by sitting in some of the trees, and I wrote this poem in support of them. I came to the campus intending to post the poem on other trees, a project swiftly frustrated by the campus police. But instead I read it at a press conference that happened to be taking place. It thus became my only poem to date to have been quoted in the San Francisco Chronicle, *the* Oakland Tribune, *the* Journal of the Berkeley Architectural Heritage Association, *as well as on TV and two dozen radio stations throughout the state of California.*

I think that I shall never see
A touchdown *lovely as a tree.*   *Kilmer*
It's great to watch kids play a game
Big Money makes it not the same.
And where Big Money is the rule
A school forgets it is a school;
Till Time, *indifferent in a week*
To a beautiful physique,   *Auden*
Will judge those schools that went to Hell
As farm teams for the NFL.

Annihilating what we made
Of *a green thought in a green shade,*   *Marvell*
The health of a society is tested
When gentle people get arrested.
Good God! I never thought to see
Poets arrested in a tree.
But, folks, if you don't heed this call
You may not see this *tree at all.*   *Nash*

AT THE ACADEMIC MEMORIAL SERVICE

Jenny clasped me as I left—briefly
my face was buried in her fragrant hair
and for a moment the hall trembled
or perhaps it was just myself that trembled
remembering her as a student long ago,
much as when Dante in Paradise
again, as in his youth, saw Beatrice
and recognized *the signs of the ancient flame.*[4]

Don't think my blessing came three decades late.
It was a privilege reserved for age—
the paradox that now one's good for little
and life is something left behind—now
for the first time such gifts
such freedoms become permissible.

Berkeley, October 13, 2013

---

4   Dante, *Purgatorio* 30:48: "Conosco i segni de l'antica fiamma;" cf. Virgil, *Aeneid* 4:23: "Agnosco veteris vestigia flammae."

WALKING ON THE DARKNESS

For Rebecca Kylie Law, the first person to initiate a Ph. D dissertation on the poetry of Peter Dale Scott

Every morning
I walk on the darkness
below Australia

and on Rebecca upside-down
on the other side
of this impenetrable earth

the first to dissect my words
no longer mine now but
for those with a different slant

though they were never truly mine
being like the rich
firmament of DNA

I have transmitted to my grandchildren
from a source older than our selves
part of some timeless process

of which we can discern
neither the beginning nor the end
so I should be thankful

they are now studied with care
under Rebecca's inverted microscope
a cockatoo at her sunny window

before she goes out to walk
on the darkness surrounding me.

AT ANGKOR WAT

The long straight walking path
from one ruined Buddhist temple to another
gave Khmer girls a quarter-hour window
to sell their postcards. One, perhaps fifteen,
glommed on to me from my left, while on my right
my daughter Cassie, a 45-year-old feminist,
kept her eyes firmly forward as we walked.

Vivacious, in an ironed blouse and skirt
with a vendor's license round her teen-age neck,
the girl spoke English heavily accented,
yet fluent and familiar enough to prove
she was well trained in selling: I was drawn
into more and more friendly conversation:
both of us teasing, laughing at our wit.

And in this light mood, as we approached
the steps up to the temple, I surprised
and shocked myself, saying, without a moment's
premeditation, and quite forcefully
so that Cassie might have overheard,
"No, I don't want your silly postcards!
I want you!"

Then as I was dealing with my terror
that I had offended both my companions,
the girl thrust aside her tray of postcards
and came up close, almost into my face,
saying, urgently, passionately, "Oh Mistair!
Meestair! *I* want *you*!"

Well! Thank goodness Cassie was beside me
to preserve from going anywhere
both her somewhat unpredictable father
and also this moment which—despite
its background of poverty and sexploitation—
I remember as meaningful:

Two strangers, from opposite sides of the world,
drawn, for a moment, to each other's eyes. . . . . .

December 24, 2004

JERUSALEM

I came to this Holy Land
of limestone and olive trees
with signs of *Armageddon*   *Megiddo*
and where people would say *Peace!*
in different languages
but then talk of revenge
I would listen and be obsessed
by how I would not respond.

We drove down into Hebron
the cold Galil rifle
of a hitch-hiking Jewish soldier
nestling against my ear
he said *It's hard on us here
always having to bust
these rock-throwing children*
and I could not reply to him.

The settler who loved the land
but commuted each day into town
was proud of their planted vineyard
and of their hopes to expand
pointed down to two Arab villages
one *OK* one *Not so good*
Who will pick your grapes? I asked
and was mute when she said she could.

Just as back in Berkeley
I would hear friends boast of their day
at the Lake Chabot rifle range
with John Birchers on their right
Black Panthers on their left
all aware they were getting ready
for the day of reckoning—-
—-I had no dog in that fight.

Here West Coast faiths are mellowed
remote from the hate and blood
exhausted years before
by decades of pain and war
there Zealots defiled the Mount
till the Romans burned it down
Is this the way of the world
and must it happen again?

Aeneas's escape
from the walls of burning Troy
to establish a new city
where no city was before
is said to have helped refine
his archaic piety
imposing peace with law   *Aeneid VI.852*
to bring the haughty low.   *Isaiah 2:17, Aeneid VI.8*

So Yochanan escaped   *Yochanan ben Zakkai*
Jerusalem's holocaust
to develop prayer and study
in lieu of sacrifice
Should we not celebrate
that faith was enhanced this way
rather than pray for return
to the slaughtering of beasts?

Something hovers over this poem
nudging me to affirm
we have glimpsed *the right path*
which is why I feel such pain
that I could not impart
what Dante had perceived—
of a different society
from the force of a *gentle heart.*   *cor gentil*

75

May we find a stronger voice
to empower the old dream
poets have always shared
of narrowing the abyss
between the truth we inherit
of Katyushas and M-16s
and *metta*—lovingkindness
the truth that has always been!

Jerusalem/Berkeley, 1997-2016

Haiku

January

TO MY DAUGHTER CASSIE SCOTT IN TORONTO

Deep Berkeley winter
    white magnolia petals
already falling

February

OLD CHERRY TREE ON CAMPUS

After fifty years
    most of your branches gone
still this flake for my sleeve

March

I RETURN TO A LATE WINTER IN NORTH HATLEY, QUEBEC

Snow falling in these woods
    Woops! Hidden ice! I crash
and my old heart glows!

April

IN MEMORY OF MY DEAD WIFE, I EMBRACE AN OLD SYCAMORE

As I kiss your bark
    I go limp you support me
I feel the sap rise

May

GRAVITY'S PARADOX

Confidently each day
     we walk on darkness
and then sleep on sunlight

June

WHERE WE ARE

Issa: This world
     is no bigger than
a dewdrop world

and yet   and yet

July

WHO WE ARE

Our self: the membrane
     between the distant galaxies
and those within

November

ABOVE THE SIERRA

Seatbelts! my Pinot trembles
     Beneath the clouds a huge
semi jackknifes

RE-ENTRY

In line with the tingling
of white lights
coming up his spine

he strove to raise himself up
through the double gateway
of Orion's dagger

to the point where they were just stars
in the spaces around him
as lost as he was

between his galaxy
and those of countless others
he will never know

and for a long time
he could no longer see
where he had come from

like a child in a blinding snowstorm
each flake a point of light
until in a greater darkness

he could no longer tell
if he was buried in their density
or they within him

MOVIE PREMIERE

To James Schamus

"For there is no mystery without dancing"—Lucian
"And we are all mortal" – John F. Kennedy, 1963

After the world movie premiere
we are ferried in buses to this great
rotunda of San Francisco City Hall
where just a few minutes ago we saw
the tormented image of Dan White
stalking Mayor Moscone and Harvey Milk
to the music of *Tosca*

Gently intoxicated from two Camparis
and surrounded by a dark sea
of literally hundreds
of stolid gay men in business suits and ties
while still in my dirty old straw hat
I wore this afternoon in the Castro
to protect against any more basal skin cancers

I rise to what I might not dare if sober
and dance with a tiny clutch of beautiful women
one of whom I see the next day
from the front page photo in the *Chronicle*
is Sean Penn's wife
and another in green whose mysterious
smile in the midst of her Bacchic abandon
engages me like Daphne's whom I adored
(from very far off) when I was fifteen

All this happiness is let's face it
just a huge ego trip
my fifteen minutes with the *glitterati*

Milk, October 28, 2008

the latest Mayor for the moment and the rich
who unlike Dan and myself have paid
a thousand bucks each for all this food

but the richest experience is this free-form dance
the dance where the ego full of itself
is lifted for moments in quiet joy
above its usual frontiers
that same inner force that directs poems
guiding my movements into something shared

    a glimpse
    of the erotic mystery
    The world is one

At the Thai village by the *kwan*   *lake*
during the Loy Krathong   *harvest water festival*
I moshed with the crowds of beautiful teenagers
behind the big-rig tractors and their trailers
each ferrying the solemn retinue in white
of another district beauty queen
to the blare of hard rock and generators
the heavens filling slowly
with a trail of white hot-air lanterns   *khom fai*
lifting from where we are towards the sky
halting baskets at first   then planetlike

I danced with those teenagers
their parents and grandparents
bottles of *naam kaao* passed around   *rice liquor*
brazen mothers thrusting their shy daughters
towards this unavailable old *farang*   *westerner*
to the disgust of my good friend Pak
who as a Buddhist doesn't even drink
especially since her brother's death on a motorbike

but the monks were pressed three deep
on the deck of the village temple tower and smiling
with what I imagine could be *empathic joy*   *mudita*
they too were part of that festival
while tonight outside the Castro Theatre
on the opposite side of the barricaded street
the chilled crowds waited to watch us leave
and waved their placards *No on Eight*   *Anti-Gay Marriage Proposition.*

With Peter Coyote the Buddhist movie star
I chat about Gary Snyder in Kitkitdizze
off the grid in the high Sierra
having chosen as a rule to live outside
this great whirlpool of entropy
like Thomas Merton in Gethsemani
mindful as we all should be
how those who push wanton wars get reelected
and killing a gay man may get you five years

and I shock Dan Ellsberg on the shuttle bus
You (like Harvey Milk) *are a man of faith!*
Without assurances from a higher power
or White's frozen incrustations of belief
you have risked your life
having glimpsed what others before you glimpsed—
seekers like Lennon no less than King and Gandhi—
a better life a *novus ordo*
seclorum for which there is (not counting
the wad of folded mottos in our wallets)
so little evidence

and yet when I dance with strangers—
arm draped for a lingering instant
over warm green shoulders which in another instant
I'll never see again—
there is this inexplicable plus
my self well-nourished becomes more generous

I am lifted by this sense of being grateful
to you San Francisco city on seven hills
of gays, rednecks, Marxists, Catholics
where it is ordered we should love our neighbor
and forgive their trespasses

and to you, James! prestidigital Prospero!
who made all these imaginations happen
in the midst of our aporetic rough world
we are in not of
but born to enjoy

as we awaken   very slowly
to what we cannot know

October 29, 2008

ACKNOWLEDGMENTS

Many people have helped me edit these poems and this book: my poetry group of many years (in particular Chana Bloch, Alan Williamson, Sandra Gilbert, and Beverley Bie Brahic), my friends Freeman Ng, Anna Sun, Brian Sentes, and Jim Reid, and my inspired and painstaking editors at Sheep Meadow Press, Stanley Moss and Greg Miller.

My biggest debt, as in all my books of the last two decades, is to my wife, Ronna Kabatznick.

"Cloud-rich" was published in Dhamma Moon. Fall 2016.

"Language Death" was published in *Consequence*, Spring 2014, 98-102.

"Finchity" and "Appearances" were published in *Leaping Clear*, September 2916.

"Googling for Norbert" was published in *The Los Angeles Review*, 5 (2008), 142-44.

An earlier version of "Jerusalem" was published in *Mosaic Orpheus*, 35-39.

"Berkeley Oaks" was first published as "Call to Chancellor Birgeneau," *BAHA News*, Journal of the Berkeley Architectural Heritage Association, January 27, 2007.

"An Old Man Out After Breakfast (Morning Walk)," "Before Reading this book," "Greek Theater: Mario Savio and the Socratic Quest" were published in *Journal of Poetics Research*, 4, March 2016,

"Greek Theater" was first published on line in various stages by Freeman Ng at http://www.comingtojakarta.net/2013/02/28/greek-theater/. It is also printed as "Epilogue" in my prose book, *The American Deep State: Wall Street, Big Oil, and the Attack on U.S. Democracy* (Lanham, MD: Rowman & Littlefield, 2014, 183-90).

"Tavern Underworld," "Wild Man in the Bathroom Mirror," "Another Road," "Walking on Darkness," "At Angkor Wat," "Movie Premiere," were published in FlashPøint, Web Issue 18, Summer 2016,6http://www.flashpointmag.com/fp18_Peter_Dale_Scott_Walking_on_Darkness_Six_Poems.htm.

"The Rest of This Poem Is Not in Words" was published in *Amass* 61 [Autumn 2016], 21